ने और को

यह किताब........................की है।

लेखन - प्रिया गुप्ता
चित्रांकन - आँचल गुप्ता

Copyright © Priya Gupta, 2021

www.hindikaybol.com

All Rights Reserved.

Designed by 'www.arcreativewings.com'

No part of this publication may be reproduced, distributed, or transmitted in any form or by any means, including photocopying, recording, or other electronic or mechanical methods, without the prior written permission of the author, except in the case of brief quotations embodied in critical reviews and certain other non-commercial uses permitted by copyright law.

www.hindikaybol.com

Follow us on Facebook/ Instagram
@ hindikaybol to find out about live online classes.

ISBN 978-93-5437-006-9

For all those who love listening to and telling childhood stories.

बचपन की कहानियाँ सुनने और सुनाने वालों के लिए..

——————————————••• Priya..

रावण **को** मारा, हुआ जयगान।

हमने दिवाली मनायी ।

हमने सबको मिठाई खिलायी ।

कृष्णा **ने** मिट्टी खायी।

मुँह खोला, और मैया **को** सृष्टि दिखायी।

रंगोली **को** पाँच रंगों से बनाया।

बच्चों ने खेला छुपन-छुपाई।

बबलू को ढूँढा, धप्पा! आवाज़ आयी।

गांधी ने आवाज़ उठायी ।

गांधी ने भारत **को** आज़ादी दिलायी।

दोस्तों ने पतंग उड़ायी।

डोर **को** खींचा, पतंग लहरायी।

मैंने कर ली बहुत पढ़ाई।

आज शाम **को** खाऊँगा रस-मलाई।

A preposition is a word or phrase that connects a noun or pronoun to a verb or adjective in a sentence.

In Hindi, these words are positioned after the noun/pronoun and hence they are known as post-positions.

Did you know ?

Hindi shares the script (alphabet) with Sanskrit— the language of Ramayana, Mahabharata and the Vedas!

The postposition ने is used after the actor/doer in a sentence, called **कर्ता** (karta).

There is no word in English that replaces ने.

लड़की ने देखा - The girl saw.
मैंने खाया - I ate.

ने is only used with past tense, or things that have happened already.

Only certain verbs are preceded by ने, not all the verbs.

को

The postposition **को** is used after the object that the verb is referring to, called कर्म (karm).

लड़की **ने** माँ **को** देखा - The girl saw the mother. (Mother is the 'object of the verb' who was seen).

शाम **को** बारिश होगी - It will rain this evening (Also, **को** is used to denote a day, time or date)

पोलीस **को** बुलाओ - Call the police (Police is the 'object of the verb')

को is used in all tenses- present/past and future.

Fill in the blanks with ने/को

1. मैं.....................देखा।
2. हम.....................क्रिकेट खेला।
3. 15 अगस्त...............छुट्टी है।
4. सब.....................गाना सुना।
5. आप.....................क्या चाहिए?
6. पिता........बच्चे........उठाया।
7. मंगलवार.................दिवाली है।
8. सिया.....................किताब पढ़ी।
9. बच्चे.....................भूख लगी है।
10. तितली....................फूल पसंद है।

ANSWER KEY: 1. ने 2. ने 3. को 4. ने 5. को 6. ने, को 7. को 8. ने 9. को 10. को

Ram shot the arrow.
(He) killed Ravan, all praises for Ram.

We celebrated Diwali.
We offered sweets to everyone.

Krishna ate dirt.
He opened the mouth,
showed the universe to his mother.

Grandma decorated the porch.
She made the Rangoli with five colors.

The children played hide-n-seek.
(They) found Bablu, came the sound 'Dhappa'.

Gandhi raised his voice.
Gandhi brought India freedom.

Friends flew the kites.
They pulled the string, the kite swayed.

I have done enough reading.
I will eat Rasmalai this evening.

Vowels / स्वर (swar)

अ	आ	इ	ई	उ	ऊ	ऋ
a	aa	i	ee	u	oo	ri

ए	ऐ	ओ	औ	अं	अः
a	ae	o	au	am	ah

Consonant / व्यंजन (vyanjan)

क	ख	ग	घ	ङ
ka	kha	ga	gha	ng
च	छ	ज	झ	ञ
ca	cha	ja	jha	ña
ट	ठ	ड	ढ	ण
ṭa	ṭha	ḍa	ḍha	ṇa
त	थ	द	ध	न
ta	tha	da	dha	na
प	फ	ब	भ	म
pa	pha	ba	bha	ma

य	र	ल	व
ya	ra	la	va
श	ष	स	ह
sh	sh	sa	ha

क्ष	त्र	ज्ञ
ksh	tra	gya

www.ingramcontent.com/pod-product-compliance
Lightning Source LLC
LaVergne TN
LVHW061628070526
838199LV00070B/6623